Why Do We Worship?

Miranda Nerland

Illustrated by Hayley O'Neal

DeWard kids

Why Do We Worship?
DeWard Publishing Company, Ltd.
P.O. Box 6259, Chillicothe, Ohio 45601
800.300.9778
www.deward.com

© 2017 DeWard Publishing

Cover and interior illustrations © 2017 by Hayley O'Neal

Printed in the United States of America.

ISBN: 978-1-936341-97-9

This book is dedicated to the boy who asks all the questions. His curiosity and earnest wondering inspired every word.

It is also dedicated to all parents who hope to plant a deep and abiding love for God in their children. I hope it inspires your child to know God, consider others, and heartily engage in worship with fresh eyes and an open heart.

We worship God in many ways,
and for many reasons.

When we meet with our church family on Sundays,
we come together to worship God.

Psalm 95:6

5

Worshiping God means that we
RESPECT HIM,
PRAISE HIM,
and LEARN what
He wants us to do.
We worship because He wants us to
and because HE IS WONDERFUL!

Psalm 86:9-10

There are SO MANY REASONS to worship God!

God is big.

Isaiah 40:12

God is bigger than the things that scare us,
and bigger than the things that make us sad.

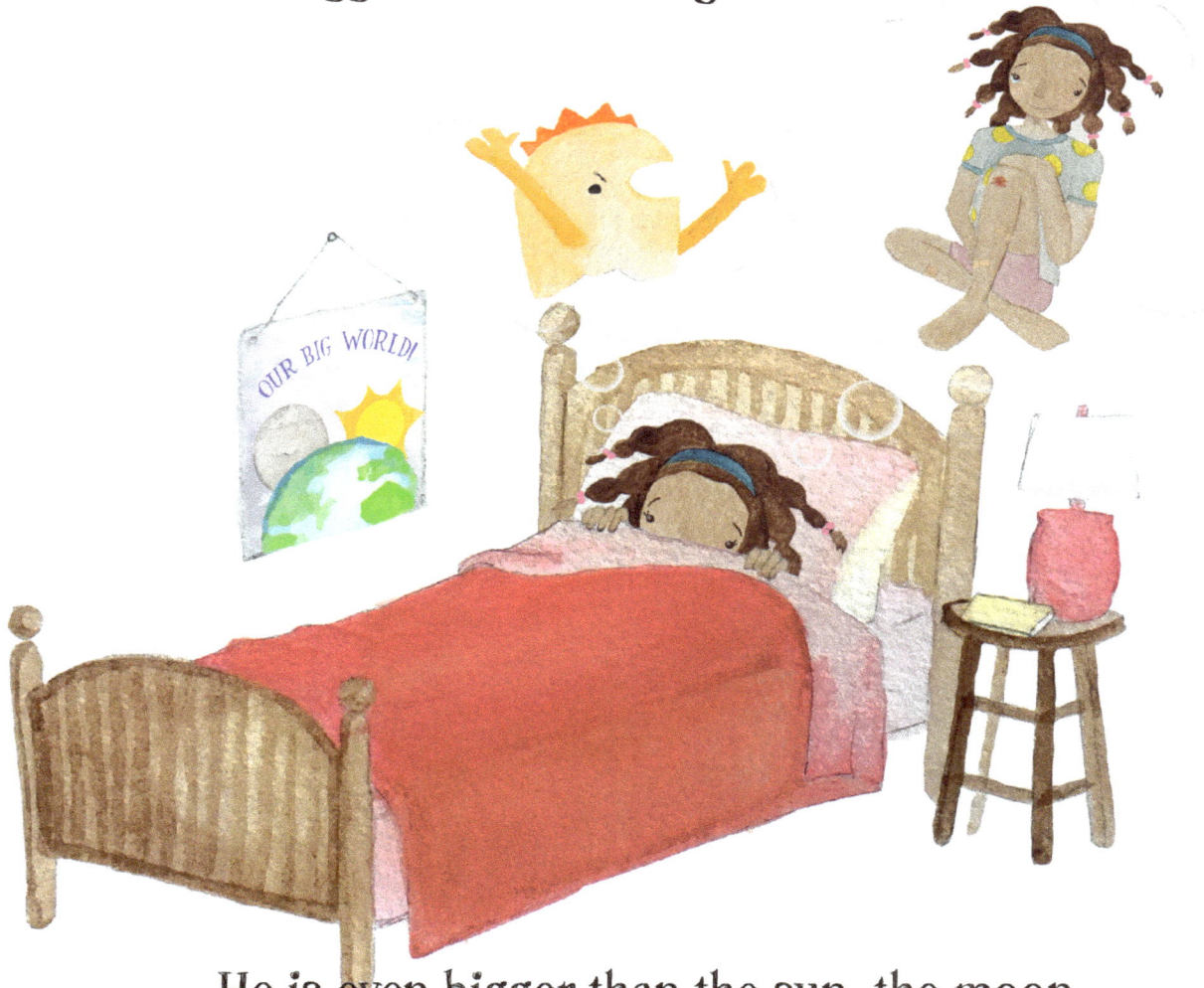

He is even bigger than the sun, the moon,
and the universe!

What is the biggest thing you can think of?

well,
God is
bigger!

God is smart.

Romans 11:33

He knows everything, and He sees everything.

He knows how many hairs are on your head
and how many grains of sand are on the beach.

Luke 12:7

God is so smart that He created the entire world
and everything in it,

and then He made it all work together just right.

God is good.

Psalm 86:5

Everywhere we look, we can see God's goodness.
It's in the sun and rain, the plants and animals,
and in our happy homes.

God made every good thing you have,
and then He shared those things with you!

And God is never bad.
He never makes a bad choice,
says a bad word, or thinks a bad thought.

He is always good.

God is strong.

He never gets sick and He never gets tired.
And there is nothing that God can't do.

Isaiah 40:28

And God is full of love.
Psalm 103:11

Even though He is so big,
God loves the littlest boys and girls.

Our smart God loves us when we do not always say the smartest things or make the smartest choices.

Our good God loves us when we do things that are not so good and when we forget to do good things for others.

Our strong God loves us when we feel weak, small, sick, and tired.

God loves us all the time and that makes us want to worship Him. We want to praise God for who He is and thank Him for what He has done for us.

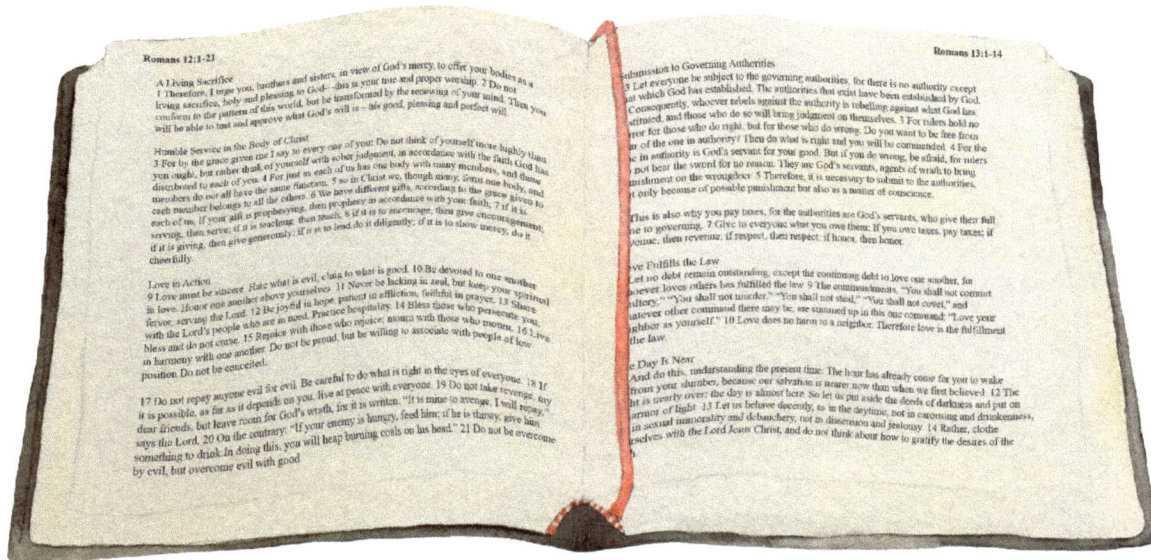

God knows that it is good for us to worship Him, so He used his wonderful Bible to tell His people just what to do when they worship.

Hebrews 12:28

The Bible tells us that God's people worshiped in the morning, and they worshiped at night. They worshiped alone, and they worshiped with others. They worshiped in temples and tents, in palaces and prisons. They worshiped everywhere, and they worshiped all the time.

Deuteronomy 6:4-7

You can worship too! You can worship when you wake up and before you go to sleep. You can worship inside or outside, morning or night. And you can worship with your friends and family every week at church.

Psalm 34:1

When you sing songs each week with
your church family, you are worshiping!
Singing helps us thank God for loving
us and giving us good things.

When you sing, you tell God how much you
love Him, and how wonderful He is.

Psalm 96:1-2

When you quietly bow your head in prayer, you are worshiping. As you pray, think about all of the things God has done. Praise Him for His goodness, and thank Him for your blessings.

God always listens when you pray, so you can tell Him anything. Tell Him about all the things that make you feel sad, scared, or frustrated. Ask Him to forgive you for choices that make Him sad. You can even pray for other people, those you love or those who need God's help.

1 Thessalonians 5:16-18

Preachers share good news from the Bible.
When we listen to the preacher's lesson, we hear
all about God's people and His wonderful plan,
and we can learn the things God wants us to know.

Sometimes it's hard to listen when you don't
know every word, but listening quietly
is one way to help others listen, too.

2 Timothy 3:16

When grown-ups take the Lord's supper, you can think about God's son Jesus and His love for you.

And when you or your parents put money in the collection plate to help God's work, remember that everything you have belongs to God.

You can even think of ways to honor God and help others with the blessings He has given you.

Proverbs 3:9

Worship shows God that you love Him, and that you want to obey Him. God is always pleased when you worship Him.

We are so blessed to have a God
who will accept
the worship we offer,
and who wants us to worship Him
in Heaven one day.

Revelation 5:11-13

DeWard kids

www.deward.com

www.ingramcontent.com/pod-product-compliance
Lightning Source LLC
Chambersburg PA
CBHW041434040426
42452CB00021B/2975